W9-AGC-533

NATIONAL GEOGRAPHIC KiDS

weird but true! 9

NATIONAL GEOGRAPHIC
KiDS

weird but true! 9

300 outrageous facts

NATIONAL GEOGRAPHIC
WASHINGTON, D.C.

HOME
SWEET
HOME

4

The planet **Venus** may have once been **habitable.**

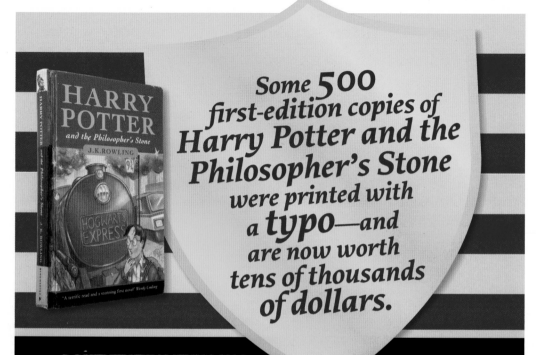

Some **500** first-edition copies of *Harry Potter and the Philosopher's Stone* were printed with a **typo**—and are now worth tens of thousands of dollars.

A SCIENTIST IN MEXICO HAS DEVELOPED THE TECHNOLOGY TO CREATE **GLOW-IN-THE-DARK SIDEWALKS.**

AN ARTIST USED **NESTS** FROM **WASPS AND HORNETS** TO CREATE A HUMAN-SIZE **SCULPTURE OF A QUEEN BEE.**

Some types of **algae** eat themselves when food is scarce.

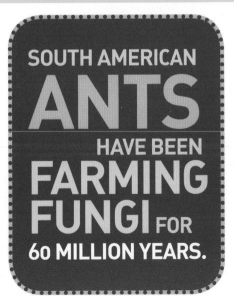

SOUTH AMERICAN **ANTS** HAVE BEEN **FARMING FUNGI** FOR 60 **MILLION YEARS.**

WHITE ADMIRAL BUTTERFLY POOP SMELLS LIKE MINT.

The
second
**new
moon**
in a
month
is called a
**black
moon.**

BLACK MOONS
OCCUR ONLY
ABOUT ONCE
EVERY 32 MONTHS.

Some
mosquitoes
prefer **cow blood**
to **human blood.**

8

9

Scientists have figured out how to...

...turn rotten **tomatoes** into **energy.**

boo!

...turn rats **transparent.**

...turn plastic trash into **fuel.**

...make a substance similar to **kryptonite.**

...create a **battery** inspired by **vitamins.**

...make a toilet that can **generate electricity** from urine.

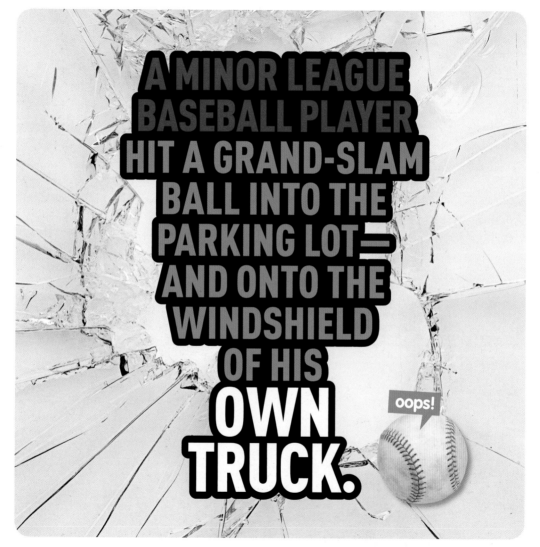

A MINOR LEAGUE BASEBALL PLAYER HIT A GRAND-SLAM BALL INTO THE PARKING LOT AND ONTO THE WINDSHIELD OF HIS OWN TRUCK.

oops!

The **metal** in one of **King Tut's daggers** was made using **iron** from a **meteorite.**

A COMPANY IN SPAIN *DEVELOPED A 3-D PRINTER THAT CAN MAKE* **PIZZA.**

TWO TEENAGERS IN WISCONSIN, U.S.A., BUILT A BACKYARD **ROLLER COASTER.**

A **pair of birds** in Angus, Scotland, regularly **steal underwear and socks** from **swimmers.**

The world's first year-round ice hotel opened in Sweden.

There are 130 species of fish that spend at least some of their time on dry land.

THE
MANCHINEEL TREE
IS SO **TOXIC** THAT EVEN
STANDING UNDER IT IN RAINY
WEATHER IS DANGEROUS.

OLYMPIC GOLD MEDALS ARE WORTH AROUND $600.

You can **swim** as fast in **syrup** as you can in **water**.

A GIANT INFLATABLE MOON ROLLED OVER TRAFFIC ON A BUSY HIGHWAY IN CHINA.

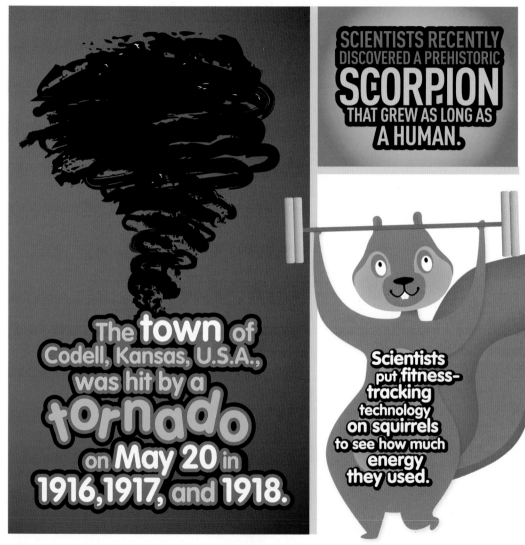

SCIENTISTS RECENTLY DISCOVERED A PREHISTORIC **SCORPION** THAT GREW AS LONG AS A HUMAN.

The **town** of Codell, Kansas, U.S.A., was hit by a **tornado** on May 20 in 1916, 1917, and 1918.

Scientists put fitness-tracking technology on squirrels to see how much energy they used.

SOME FLOWER ARRANGEMENTS IN VICTORIAN ENGLAND CONTAINED CODED MESSAGES.

GORiLLAS
SOMETIMES **SING** HAPPY SONGS WHEN THEY **EAT.**

A hotel straddling the border of France and Switzerland lets you sleep with **your head** in one country and **your feet** in the other.

THE U.S.-CANADIAN **BORDER** RUNS THROUGH THE MIDDLE OF A LIBRARY.

Some **scientists** think that most of the **universe** is trapped inside **ancient black holes.**

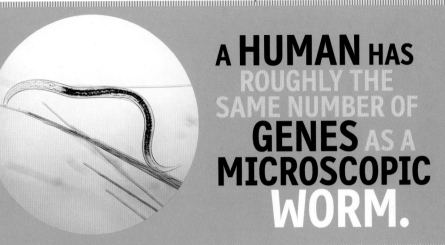

A **HUMAN** HAS ROUGHLY THE SAME NUMBER OF **GENES** AS A **MICROSCOPIC WORM.**

SCIENTISTS HAVE ENGINEERED SPINACH PLANTS THAT CAN *DETECT* BOMBS.

Every August, people in Bolivia gather to **break rocks** for **good luck.**

Sociable weavers build "apartment" nests that can house up to 500 birds.

THE COMMUNAL **NESTS** CAN **WEIGH** AS MUCH AS A SMALL **CAR.**

A BILLIONAIRE BOUGHT **EIGHT** **$1,000** SMARTPHONES— FOR HIS **DOG.**

A *whooping crane's* **eyes** *change from blue to aqua to* **gold** *as it grows older.*

Thieves in Wisconsin, U.S.A., stole 20,000 pounds (9,072 kg) of cheese.

SCIENTISTS USED **BACTERIA** TO MAKE A **MICROSCOPIC** WIND FARM.

There are decomposed **wasps** inside of figs.

Flat millipedes shoot a defensive spray that smells like cherry cola.

33

THERE'S A SCULPTURE AS TALL AS A GIRAFFE SITTING ON THE OCEAN FLOOR IN THE BAHAMAS.

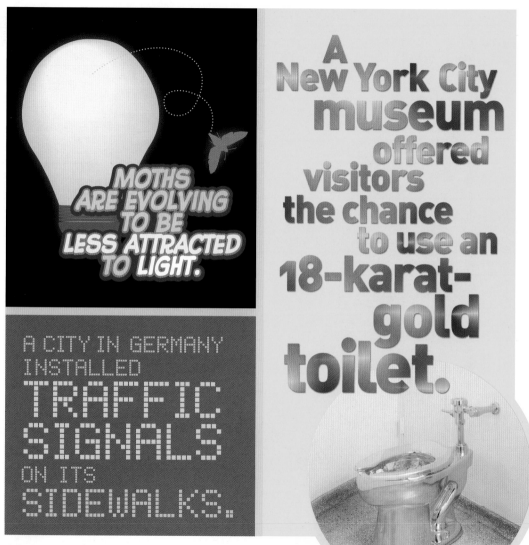

MOTHS ARE EVOLVING TO BE LESS ATTRACTED TO LIGHT.

A CITY IN GERMANY INSTALLED TRAFFIC SIGNALS ON ITS SIDEWALKS.

A New York City museum offered visitors the chance to use an 18-karat-gold toilet.

THE CONTINENT OF AUSTRALIA MOVES BACK AND FORTH WHEN THE SEASONS CHANGE.

AUSTRALIA HAS DRIFTED ALMOST FIVE FEET (1.5 m) NORTH IN THE PAST 22 YEARS.

IN TAIWAN, IT'S TRENDY TO GET YOUR DOG'S FUR GROOMED INTO GEOMETRIC SHAPES.

COFFEE JELLY— A JIGGLY DESSERT MADE FROM **ESPRESSO—** IS A POPULAR **DESSERT** IN JAPAN.

BLACK HOLES "EAT" STARS AND "BURP" GAS.

Researchers observed a **sea lion** named **Ronan** bobbing her head in time with **music.**

SOME BIRDS "TALK" TO THEIR UNHATCHED EGGS.

DOGS CAN UNDERSTAND HUMAN SPEECH.

41

Leonardo da Vinci may have written backward

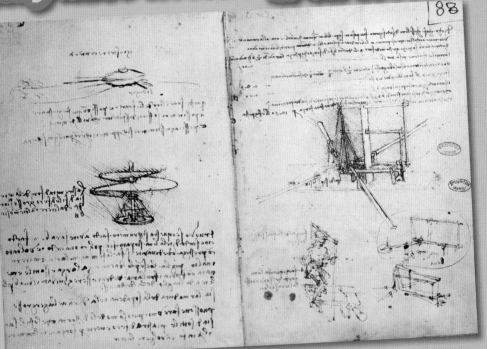

to keep people from stealing his ideas.

A MAN RODE A **UNICYCLE** AROUND AN **840-FOOT-TALL** (256-m) **CHIMNEY** IN ROMANIA.

Chork= chopsticks **+** fork

A man accidentally discovered a **49,000-year-old** human settlement while taking a **bathroom break** in an Australian park.

43

The pop-up **Museum** of **Ice Cream** in New York City featured a swimmable **pool** full of faux **rainbow sprinkles.**

DRAGONFLIES CAN LIVE UNDERWATER FOR TWO YEARS.

SCIENTISTS HAVE DISCOVERED HOW TO 3-D PRINT HUMAN BONE AND TISSUE.

THERE ARE AS MANY STRANDS OF CORN SILK AS THERE ARE KERNELS ON THE COB.

45

A family in New Jersey, U.S.A., lives in a farmhouse encased in an aircraft hangar.

FRESHWATER SNAILS KILL

MORE HUMANS EVERY YEAR

THAN DO LIONS, WOLVES, CROCODILES, AND SHARKS COMBINED.

Some piranhas are vegetarian.

THE LAWS OF PHYSICS DO NOT RULE OUT TIME TRAVEL..

You can buy a smartphone case that looks like an ice-cream sandwich.

Early ketchup recipes included mushrooms, oysters, and walnuts— but no tomatoes.

A NEW SPECIES OF TROPICAL ANT WAS RECENTLY DISCOVERED IN A FROG'S BELLY.

It costs the **U.S. Mint** about **eight cents** to make **one nickel.**

Benjamin Franklin invented a glass harmonica.

THE FIRST ANIMALS LAUNCHED INTO OUTER SPACE? **FRUIT FLIES.**

Diamondback rattlesnakes can **strike** in about half the time it takes you to **blink.**

An **artist** created the world's largest **biodegradable portrait** on a grassy slope in Switzerland.

Scientists recently discovered a glowing purple blob on the floor of the Pacific Ocean.

A FAST-FOOD RESTAURANT ONCE GAVE AWAY FRIED-CHICKEN-SCENTED SUNSCREEN.

A 31-YEAR-OLD **CRIMINAL** WAS ABLE TO EVADE **POLICE** FOR MONTHS BY DISGUISING HIMSELF **AS AN OLD MAN.**

THE **U.S.** STATES OF ALASKA AND HAWAII HAVE THE SAME RECORD-HIGH TEMPERATURE: **100°F.** (37.8°C)

AN ARTIST IN PHILADELPHIA, PENNSYLVANIA, U.S.A., CREATES ART USING DISCARDED CANDY WRAPPERS.

COCKROACHES ARE MORE LIKELY TO FLY IN HOT WEATHER.

THE PACIFIC BEETLE COCKROACH

58

Cockroaches have a built-in GPS!

HEY, GUYS, WAIT UP!

PRODUCES MILK.

COCKROACH MILK IS MORE NUTRITIOUS THAN COW'S MILK.

A PAIR OF TOURISTS RECENTLY DISCOVERED

400-YEAR-OLD

ROCK CARVINGS

ON A HAWAIIAN BEACH.

It was once believed that massaging ground-up **pumpkin** onto your face could remove **freckles.**

A man in New York, U.S.A., returned a **library book** that was **15,531 days** (that's 42 years!) **overdue.**

DIVERS EXPLORING A SHIPWRECK OFF THE COAST OF SWEDEN FOUND A HUNK OF 340-YEAR-OLD CHEESE INSIDE A SEALED CONTAINER.

The oldest known **orca**—nicknamed "Granny"— lived to be 105.

Firefighting was an unofficial event at the 1900 Summer Olympics in Paris, France.

THE VIDEO GAME CHARACTER **MARIO** WAS ORIGINALLY NAMED **JUMPMAN.**

MINIATURE BLACK HOLES MAY BE

PASSING THROUGH EARTH EVERY DAY, A STUDY FOUND.

TEN PERCENT
OF THE WORLD'S
REDHEADS
LIVE IN
IRELAND.

Ireland
is about the size of
South Carolina,
U.S.A.

A 1,075-year-old pine tree in Greece is the oldest known living thing in Europe.

SOME RATTLESNAKES IN THE GRAND CANYON ARE PINK.

A mouse scurrying through displays at the Museum of English Rural Life in Great Britain got caught in a 155-year-old mousetrap.

SEA STARS DON'T HAVE BLOOD.

Great frigate birds can fly for two months straight without landing.

THEY **NAP** WHILE THEY'RE FLYING.

SCIENTISTS THINK THAT BOTH **REPTILES** AND **BIRDS** MAY **DREAM** WHILE SLEEPING.

SOME **COLD VIRUSES** ORIGINATED IN **CAMELS.**

NEED A TISSUE?

THE EARTH'S SURFACE IS TWO AND A HALF YEARS OLDER THAN ITS CORE.

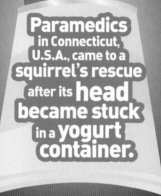

Paramedics in Connecticut, U.S.A., came to a **squirrel's rescue** after its **head** **became stuck** in a **yogurt container.**

JELLYFISH EAT AND POOP THROUGH THE SAME OPENING.

A **bakery** in London sells a **doughnut** topped with caviar, gold leaf, gold vanilla beans, and a rare type of chocolate. *The price tag?* £1,500, or about $2,000.

A friendly **stray dog** followed an **ultramarathon runner** for **77 miles** (124 km) in China's Gobi desert.

HOW'S MY PACE?

Chameleon spit is 400 times thicker than human spit.

SCIENTISTS USED A **3-D PRINTER** TO MAKE **A PROSTHETIC BEAK** FOR A GOOSE MISSING MOST OF HER BILL.

A NEW YORK RESTAURANT **SERVES PIZZA IN A BOX**

MADE OF PIZZA.

When a **bee stings,** it releases a chemical that smells like **bananas.**

THE GAS VOLUME OF A **LARGE TOOT** COULD FILL A SODA CAN.

Underwater volcanoes cover more of the Earth than deserts or tundras.

THREE-TOED SLOTHS BURN ONLY 110 CALORIES A DAY—ABOUT THE SAME AS A HUMAN PLAYING SOCCER FOR 10 MINUTES.

Some **stray cows** in India have been fitted with **glow-in-the-dark bands** around their horns so drivers can spot them at night.

BOO!

PARTS OF **BEIJING, CHINA,** ARE **SINKING** BY UP TO **FOUR INCHES** (10.2 cm) A YEAR, A STUDY SHOWED.

Most **kangaroos** are left-handed.

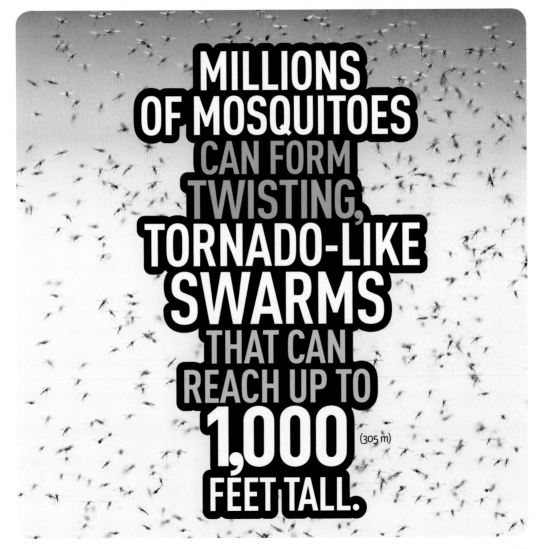

MILLIONS OF MOSQUITOES CAN FORM TWISTING, TORNADO-LIKE SWARMS THAT CAN REACH UP TO 1,000 (305 m) FEET TALL.

JANUARY 14 IS DRESS UP YOUR PET DAY.

NEVER FORCE YOUR PET TO DO OR WEAR ANYTHING IT DOESN'T WANT TO.

SCIENTISTS TRAINED **HORSES** TO COMMUNICATE WITH PEOPLE USING *SYMBOLS.*

HORSE HOOVES NEVER STOP GROWING.

CORAL REEFS THRIVE.

DØDSING=
BELLY FLOPPING OFF
A THREE-STORY-TALL
PLATFORM

IT HAS SNOWED IN THE SAHARA.

RESEARCHERS ONCE CONDUCTED A STUDY ON THE PERSONALITIES OF ROCKS.

Toads don't have teeth (but frogs do).

A mama moose gave birth to a calf in a shopping center parking lot in Anchorage, Alaska, U.S.A.

www.bigidahopotato.com

A BIG HELPING

The Famous Idaho Potato Tour

YOU'LL KNOW
IT'S REAL
When You See the Seal!

A **SIX-TON** (5.4-t) "**POTATO**" FLOATED ON A BARGE ALONG A RIVER IN NEW YORK, U.S.A.

You can go to elf school in Reykjavík, Iceland.

0.001 PERCENT OF YOUR **TAN** COMES FROM PHOTONS LEFT OVER FROM THE **BIG BANG.**

The Royal Norwegian Guard promoted a **penguin** *named Sir Nils Olav III* to **brigadier,** *one of its* **highest honors.**

Invisible poems
were painted on
sidewalks
in Boston, Massachusetts, U.S.A.

MY NOTES THE W

SNOW H

LOOKS LIKE BETWEEN 'EM THEY DONE

TRIED TO MAKE ME

STOP LAUGHIN' STOP LOVIN' STOP LIVIN'

BUT I DON'T CARE!

I'M STILL HERE!

HU S

YOU CAN SEE THEM
ONLY WHEN THE
GROUND GETS WET.

The Eiffel Tower
seems smaller if you
lean left while looking at it.

FARMERS IN SUNDERLAND, MASSACHUSETTS, U.S.A., DESIGNED A **CORN MAZE** INSPIRED BY THE NOVEL ALICE'S ADVENTURES IN WONDERLAND.

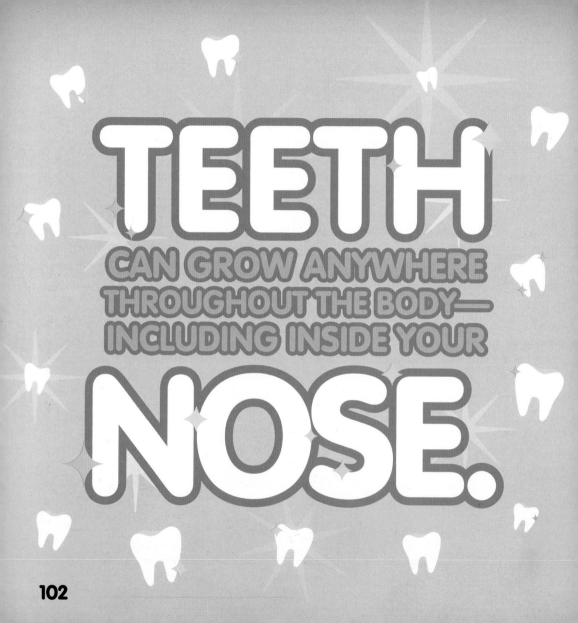

TEETH
CAN GROW ANYWHERE THROUGHOUT THE BODY—INCLUDING INSIDE YOUR
NOSE.

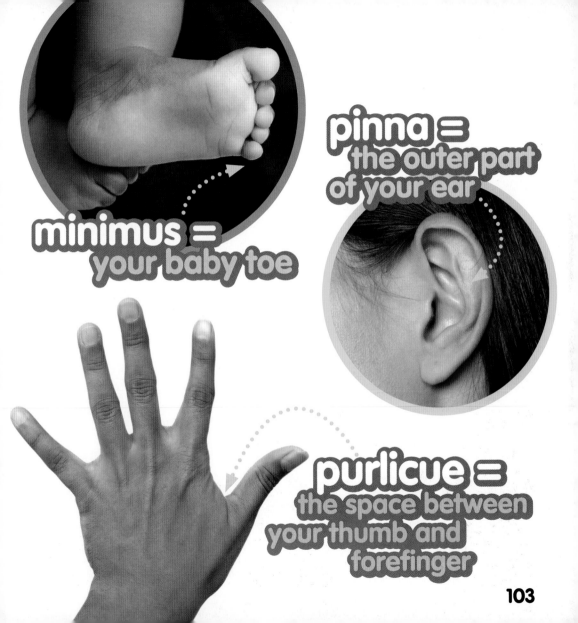

minimus = your baby toe

pinna = the outer part of your ear

purlicue = the space between your thumb and forefinger

103

SOME SPECIES OF **MICROBES** IN YOUR GUT HAVE BEEN EVOLVING **FOR MILLIONS OF YEARS.**

oops!

A MONKEY TRIGGERED A NATIONWIDE BLACKOUT AFTER TRIPPING A TRANSFORMER ON THE ROOF OF A POWER PLANT IN KENYA.

A ranch in Texas, U.S.A., is two-thirds the size of Rhode Island.

YOU CAN BUY **FRESH EGGS** FROM **VENDING MACHINES** IN JAPAN.

A **DOG** NAMED **DUKE** IS THE **MAYOR OF CORMORANT, MINNESOTA, U.S.A.**

Scientists use **rainbows** to study air pollution.

One hundred years ago, New York City **taxi cabs** were painted **green and red**, not **yellow.**

SWEET TREATS MAKE BEES FEEL OPTIMISTIC, ONE STUDY FOUND.

A MAN DRESSED AS **DARTH VADER** WAS SPOTTED PICKING UP **TRASH** ALONGSIDE A HIGHWAY IN VIRGINIA, U.S.A.

A BREED OF WOLVES LIVING ON CANADA'S VANCOUVER ISLAND CAN SWIM UP TO 7.5 MILES (12 km) TO TRACK PREY.

A species of praying mantis was named after U.S. Supreme Court justice Ruth Bader Ginsburg.

A popular fast-food restaurant in India sells chicken inside a container that can charge your cell phone.

FRUIT FLIES CAN SUFFER FROM INSOMNIA.

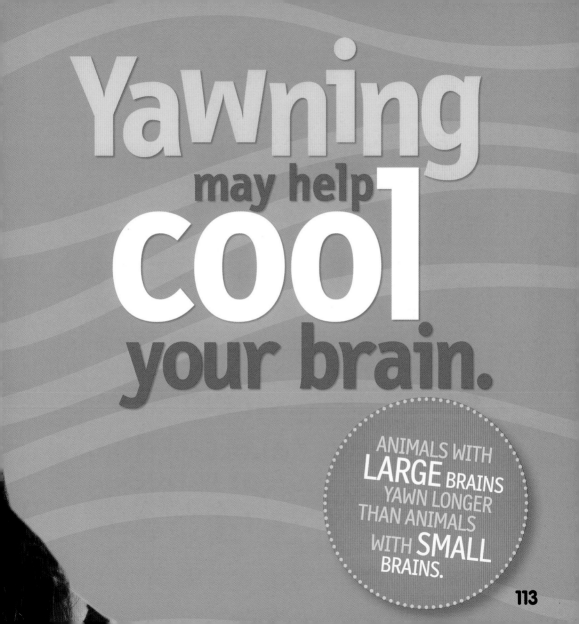

Yawning
may help
cool
your brain.

ANIMALS WITH **LARGE** BRAINS YAWN LONGER THAN ANIMALS WITH **SMALL** BRAINS.

A **BEAR** IN NEW MEXICO, U.S.A., **HITCHED A RIDE** ON TOP OF A **GARBAGE TRUCK** FOR **FIVE MILES** BEFORE CLIMBING OFF.

(8 km)

During the **world's longest race,** runners cover almost **60 miles** (97 km) **a day for 52 days.**

A small swimming snail known as a **sea butterfly** flaps its tiny wings to move through the water.

snotbot:
A ROBOT THAT COLLECTS WHALE SNOT FOR STUDY

A BLUE HOLE NEARLY AS DEEP AS THE HEIGHT OF THE EMPIRE STATE BUILDING WAS RECENTLY DISCOVERED IN THE SOUTH CHINA SEA.

MOST ANIMALS DON'T CHEW THEIR FOOD.

SCOTLAND'S NATIONAL ANIMAL IS A UNICORN.

According to researchers in Australia, **eating bananas** can make **human toots** less smelly.

petrichor = the smell in the **air** following **rain**

DON'T TRY THIS AT HOME!

One **summer,** residents of **Philadelphia,** Pennsylvania, U.S.A., swam in Dumpster **"pools"** to beat the heat.

121

CHICKENS ARE GENETICALLY CLOSER TO DINOSAURS THAN THEY ARE TO OTHER BIRDS.

Pacu fish crack open seeds and nuts with their humanlike teeth.

SEABIRD POOP *HELPS KEEP THE ARCTIC CLIMATE* **COOL.**

Tossing a **ball** of **aluminum** **foil** in your dryer can fight **static** electricity.

A *suit of armor* for a *guinea pig—* complete with a jacket and tiny helmet— sold online for more than **$24,000.**

A SINGLE **LAKE** IN SIBERIA CONTAINS **ONE-FIFTH** OF ALL THE **FRESHWATER** IN THE WORLD.

A **giraffe** can clean its **nose** with its **tongue.**

THE LONGEST-LASTING LIGHTNING BOLT EVER RECORDED WAS 7.74 SECONDS.

SPIDERS HEAR WITH THEIR LEGS.

A chef in New York City created a **doughnut** made from **purple yams** and dipped in **edible gold.**

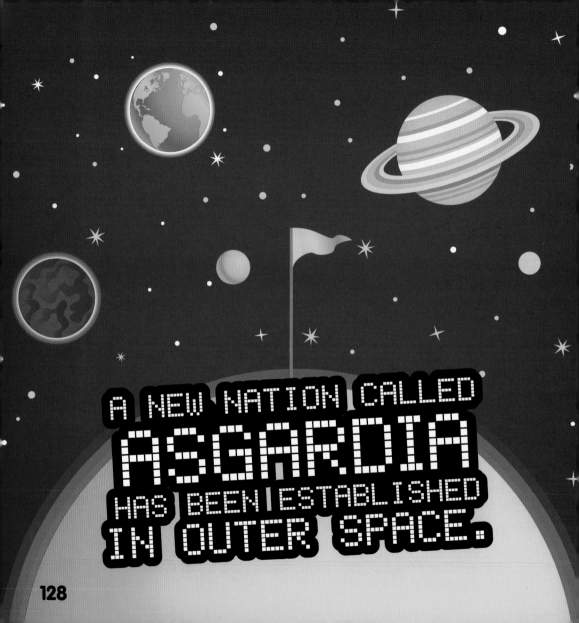

A NEW NATION CALLED **ASGARDIA** HAS BEEN ESTABLISHED IN OUTER SPACE.

RESEARCHERS RECENTLY FOUND INTACT **2,000-**YEAR-OLD **HUMAN REMAINS** ON A **SHIPWRECK** OFF THE COAST OF **GREECE.**

AT BIRTH, A GIANT PACIFIC OCTOPUS **IS ABOUT THE SIZE OF A** MOSQUITO.

The smallest mammal ever —**a prehistoric rodent**— was as big as your fingernail and weighed no more than a dollar bill.

Baby **jackals** eat their parents' **vomit.**

THE FOREST CANOPY IN THE AMAZON IS SO THICK THAT IT CAN TAKE 10 MINUTES FOR RAIN TO REACH FROM THE TOP OF THE TREES TO THE GROUND.

THE BLUE COLOR USED IN JEANS MAY DATE BACK 6,000 YEARS.

A WATER BUG NATIVE TO SOUTHEAST ASIA

CAN GROW AS BIG AS YOUR PALM.

A CHICKEN NAMED PATRICK PLAYS THE PIANO BY PECKING THE KEYS WITH HIS BEAK.

A HONEYBEE CAN LIFT ABOUT **80 PERCENT OF ITS** BODY WEIGHT IN POLLEN.

WHALES CAN TASTE ONLY SALTY FOODS.

Some **hermit crabs** use discarded **trash** as **shells.**

Residents of Green Bank, West Virginia, U.S.A., can't use **Wi-Fi** because of a **high-tech** government **telescope** located there.

RADIOS AND CELL PHONES ARE ALSO **BANNED.**

TURTLES MAY HAVE FIRST EVOLVED SHELLS TO HELP THEM BURROW INTO THE EARTH.

Researchers have developed **edible packaging** for food.

99 PERCENT
OF MICROBE SPECIES
HAVE NOT YET BEEN DISCOVERED,
SCIENTISTS ESTIMATE.

THE SIZE OF A LARGE PIZZA, THE **COIN** WEIGHS **220 POUNDS.** (100 kg)

CANADA HAS PRODUCED A
MILLION-DOLLAR COIN.

City bees pollinate more plants than **country bees** do, a study found.

Pumpkins are 90 percent water.

IN SPAIN, THE TOOTH *FAIRY* IS A *MOUSE* NAMED *PÉREZ.*

SCIENTISTS MADE TEMPORARY TATTOOS THAT CAN BE USED TO CONTROL SMARTPHONES.

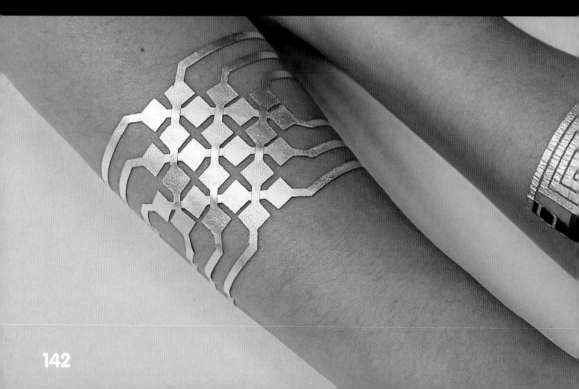

A **cat** once co-authored **a physics paper.**

SOME ANCIENT MUMMIES HAVE BEEN FOUND WITH MUMMIFIED HEAD LICE.

THERE IS AN ASTEROID SHAPED LIKE A DOG BONE.

Some **trees** know when their **branches** have been **nibbled by an animal.**

SCIENTISTS DISCOVERED A NEW **SPIDER** SPECIES THAT **LOOKS LIKE A** DRIED-UP **LEAF.**

There's a huge heart-shaped ice patch on the surface of Pluto.

Coral reef–dwelling fish can see colors that humans can't.

Hot, dry weather caused piles of **horse poop** to **burst into flames** outside a **stable** in upstate New York, U.S.A.

THE POLICE HEADQUARTERS KNOWN AS

SCOTLAND YARD IS NOT IN SCOTLAND.

Female donkeys are called **jennys.** Males are called **jacks.**

Scientists built an engine small enough to fit inside a **human cell.**

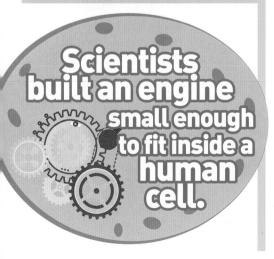

HELLO, MY NAME IS
Jenny

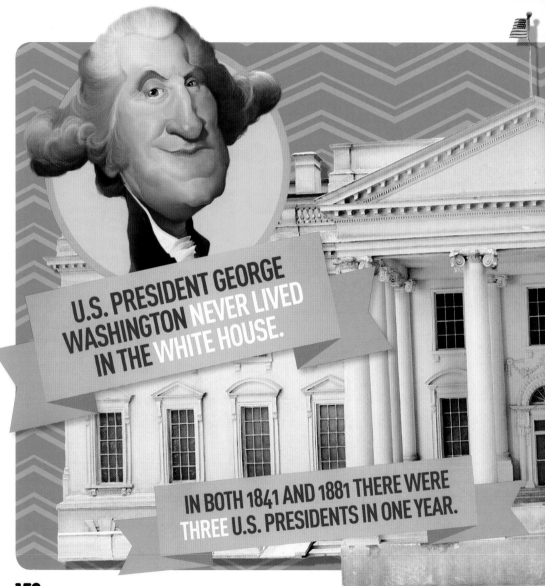

U.S. PRESIDENT GEORGE WASHINGTON NEVER LIVED IN THE WHITE HOUSE.

IN BOTH 1841 AND 1881 THERE WERE THREE U.S. PRESIDENTS IN ONE YEAR.

THERE'S A FLOWER SHOP, A CHOCOLATE SHOP, AND A BOWLING ALLEY IN THE WHITE HOUSE BASEMENT.

An elephant's brain weighs more than a two-month-old baby.

WATER BEETLES MAKE **HOMES** IN ELEPHANT FOOTPRINTS.

A pet dog named Keon has a record-setting tail that's as long as a skateboard.

Q is the only letter of the alphabet that does not appear in the name of any U.S. state.

A man in Florida, U.S.A., robbed a farmers market while wearing **a tutu.**

AT A CONTEST IN SLOVAKIA, **GRAVE DIGGERS** GO SHOVEL TO SHOVEL TO SEE WHO CAN DIG THE FASTEST— AND TIDIEST— **GRAVE.**

Catfish whiskers are known as **barbells.**

There's a contest to come up with the worst sound in the world.

Submissions included the sounds of **chili** being **stirred** and **nails** on a chalkboard.

A **600-POUND** (272-kg)
OCTOPUS
CAN SQUEEZE
THROUGH AN
OPENING THE SIZE OF A
QUARTER.

SCIENTISTS NICKNAMED A PATCH OF UNUSUALLY WARM PACIFIC OCEAN WATER "THE BLOB."

Cookie Monster said his name used to be Sid.

Scientists found a huge **lake** under a **volcano** in Bolivia.

SOME **BIRDS' BEAKS HAVE BUILT-IN AIR CONDITIONERS.**

A giant anteater flicks its tongue in and out of its mouth up to 150 times per minute.

An **ice-cream shop** in England is testing using a **drone** to deliver its **treats** to customers.

Nine-banded **armadillos** almost always give birth to identical **quadruplets.**

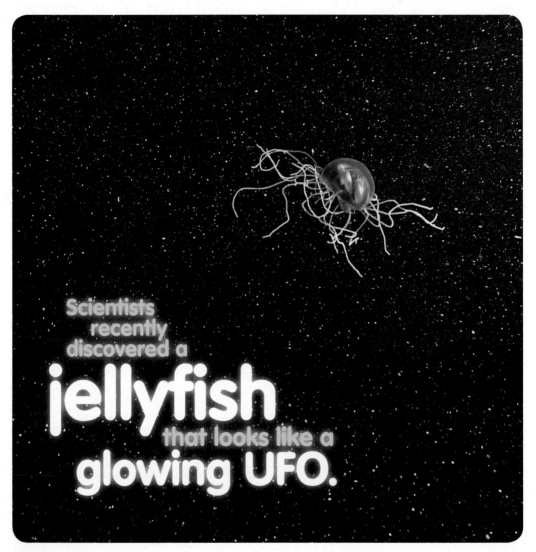

Scientists recently discovered a **jellyfish** that looks like a **glowing UFO.**

HUNDREDS OF **STRAY CATS**
ROAM AROUND DISNEYLAND, IN
CALIFORNIA, U.S.A., AT NIGHT
TO CATCH **REAL-LIFE MICE.**

A large green **snake** stowed away on **a plane** **flying** to Mexico City.

A **TEEN** IN WASHINGTON STATE, U.S.A., ONCE GOT HER **HEAD** STUCK INSIDE A GIANT **PUMPKIN.**

DON'T TRY THIS AT HOME!

THE **SKIN** OF ONE KIND OF SMALL AMAZONIAN **FROG** IS COVERED WITH **ANT** REPELLENT.

PLANTS MAY GROW FASTER IF YOU PLAY MUSIC FOR THEM.

YOU CAN EAT A MEAL

IN AN AIRPLANE-THEMED RESTAURANT—

INSIDE AN ACTUAL PLANE— IN WUHAN, CHINA.

THE **FIRST WOMAN** TO RUN FOR **U.S. PRESIDENT** RAN **BEFORE** WOMEN COULD **VOTE.**

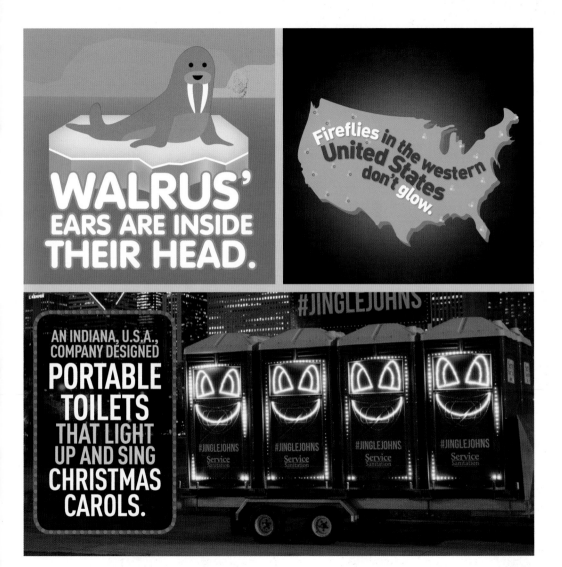

WALRUS' EARS ARE INSIDE THEIR HEAD.

Fireflies in the western United States don't glow.

AN INDIANA, U.S.A., COMPANY DESIGNED PORTABLE TOILETS THAT LIGHT UP AND SING CHRISTMAS CAROLS.

#JINGLEJOHNS

A **beach** in Siberia was once covered with hundreds of **snowballs** naturally formed by **wind** and **icy water.**

Civil War–era
cannonballs
washed up on a
South Carolina,
U.S.A., **beach** after
a hurricane.

IT COULD TAKE **300 years** TO DISCOVER EVERY SPECIES OF **tree** IN THE Amazon rain forest.

Some birds use **"baby talk"** when singing to chicks.

goo-goo   ga-ga

A couple tied the knot during a roller coaster ride in North Carolina, U.S.A.

Each year, Americans throw away some $60 million in loose change.

Only 8 percent of U.S. money is paper and coins (the rest is just numbers on a computer).

A NEW YORK MAN CREATED A **VIDEO-GAME-THEMED HALLOWEEN COSTUME** THAT PLAYS AN ACTUAL VIDEO GAME.

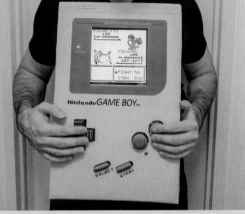

A **HUNTSMAN SPIDER** CAN GROW AS BIG AS A **DINNER PLATE.**

GORILLAS CAN CATCH HUMAN COLDS.

FISH CALLED SKATES CAN SEE ONLY IN BLACK AND WHITE.

U.S. PRESIDENT BARACK OBAMA ONCE WORKED AT AN ICE-CREAM SHOP.

YOU CAN ORDER SCOOPS OF PEAR-AND-BLUE-CHEESE-FLAVORED ICE CREAM AT A SHOP IN PORTLAND, OREGON, U.S.A.

ASPARAGUS, OYSTER, AND PARMESAN CHEESE WERE POPULAR ICE-CREAM FLAVORS IN THE UNITED STATES IN THE 18TH IN THE CENTURY.

An **Italian man** piled **121 scoops** of ice cream onto one cone.

A **hotel** in the Grand Canyon Caverns is 220 feet underground.

(67 m)

Northern stargazer fish zap their predators with a jolt of electricity.

Road **noise** from nearby **highways** can make it hard for some animals to **sniff out** predators.

A FOSSIL HUNTER IN THE U.K. FOUND A "**PICKLED**" DINOSAUR BRAIN.

THOUSANDS OF YEARS AGO, SOME PEOPLE CARRIED WATER AROUND IN **HOLLOWED OSTRICH EGGS.**

MICE CAN FEEL EACH **other's pain.**

A **FLOCK** OF **FLYING** **WiLD** TURKEYS CAUSED POWER OUTAGES IN AN OREGON, U.S.A., TOWN.

DUNG BEETLES TAKE MENTAL "SNAPSHOTS" OF THE NIGHT SKY.

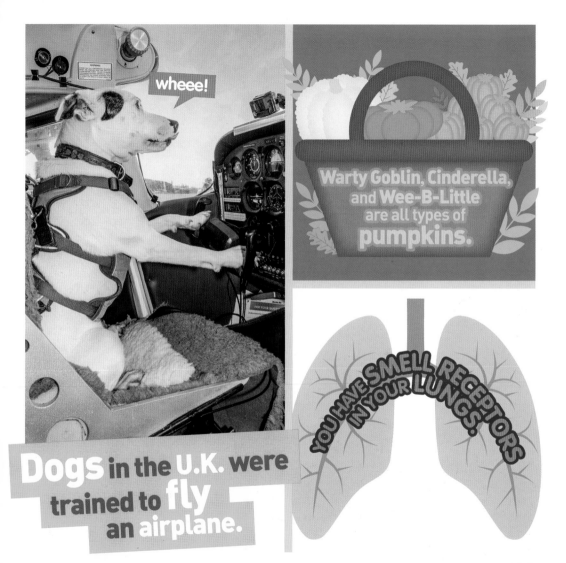

wheee!

Warty Goblin, Cinderella, and **Wee-B-Little** are all types of **pumpkins.**

Dogs in the U.K. were trained to **fly** an airplane.

YOU HAVE SMELL RECEPTORS IN YOUR LUNGS.

SOME
DINOSAURS HAD FOREST-CAMOUFLAGE COLORING.

THE FIRST MODERN COMPUTER WEIGHED 30 TONS.
(27 t)

RESEARCHERS FOUND THAT RATS THAT LISTENED TO MOZART LEARNED TO RUN MAZES FASTER THAN RATS THAT LISTENED TO OTHER MUSIC.

SOME **FROG CALLS** CAN BE HEARD UP TO A MILE AWAY.

(1.6 km)

A baby echidna is called a puggle.

TREES "SLEEP" AT NIGHT.

RESEARCHERS HAVE FOUND A WAY TO USE SEWAGE TO MAKE FUEL.

Tadpoles eat **vegetarian meals** during heat waves.

Dog fleas jump higher than cat fleas.

U.S. TOWNS AND CITIES WITH THE

Good Grief, Idaho

IDAHO

SOUTH DAKOTA

Plenty Bears, South Dakota

CALIFORNIA

Zzzyzx, California

TEXAS

Ding Dong, Texas

STRANGEST NAMES INCLUDE...

Goobertown,
Arkansas

Lizard Lick,
North Carolina

Boar Tush, Alabama

NORTH
CAROLINA

ARKANSAS

ALABAMA

FACTFINDER

Boldface indicates illustrations.

FACTFINDER

FACTFINDER

Copyright © 2017 National Geographic Partners, LLC

Published by National Geographic Partners, LLC. All rights reserved. Reproduction of the whole or any part of the contents without written permission from the publisher is prohibited.

Since 1888, the National Geographic Society has funded more than 12,000 research, exploration, and preservation projects around the world. The Society receives funds from National Geographic Partners, LLC, funded in part by your purchase. A portion of the proceeds from this book supports this vital work. To learn more, visit natgeo.com/info.

NATIONAL GEOGRAPHIC and Yellow Border Design are trademarks of the National Geographic Society, used under license.

For more information, visit nationalgeographic.com, call 1-800-647-5463, or write to the following address:

National Geographic Partners
1145 17th Street N.W.
Washington, D.C. 20036-4688 U.S.A.

Visit us online at nationalgeographic.com/books

For librarians and teachers: ngchildrensbooks.org

More for kids from National Geographic: kids.nationalgeographic.com

For information about special discounts for bulk purchases, please contact National Geographic Books Special Sales: specialsales@natgeo.com

For rights or permissions inquiries, please contact National Geographic Books Subsidiary Rights: bookrights@natgeo.com

Designed by Rachael Hamm Plett, Moduza Design

Trade paperback ISBN: 978-1-4263-2893-0
Reinforced library binding ISBN:
978-1-4263-2894-7

Printed in China
17/PPS/1

The publisher would like to thank Jen Agresta, project editor; Avery Hurt, researcher and author; and Sarah Wassner Flynn, researcher and author.

PHOTO CREDITS

All artwork by MODUZA DESIGN unless otherwise noted below:

ASP = Alamy Stock Photo; GI = Getty Images; SS = Shutterstock

Cover, Kuttelvaserova Stuchelova/SS; Spine, Kuttelvaserova Stuchelova/SS; 2, Kuttelvaserova Stuchelova/SS; 4, NASA/JPL; 6, Heritage Auctions, Dallas; 7 (LE), Ed Reschke/GI; 8 (UP), Gerald A. DeBoer/SS; 9, Queensland Museum, Austrailia; 9 (LO RT), Michiel de Wit/SS; 10-11 (Background), bimka/SS; 10 (CTR LE), Maxim Petrichuk/SS; 10 (CTR RT), De Jongh Photography/SS; 10 (LO CTR), alterfalter/SS; 11 (UP), Jasony00/Dreamstime; 11 (CTR), Maxx-Studio/SS; 11 (LO), Nikola Spasenoski/SS; 12, Celiafoto/SS; 12 (LO RT), Bryan Solomon/SS; 13 (UP), François Guene/Art Resource, NY; 13 (LO RT), Dave Deaven; 15, Arctic-Images/GI; 16, Nicholas Toh/ASP; 18, Amy Toensing/National Geographic Creative; 23, Sanjaykj/Dreamstime; 27 (UP), NNehring/GI; 28, Anna Morgan/SS; 29, Danita Delimont/GI; 30 (LE), Bilevich Olga/SS; 30 (RT), 4harmony/Dreamstime; 33 (LE), oriori/SS; 34, Jason deCaires Taylor. All rights reserved, DACS/ARS 2017, Photo: Jason deCaires Taylor; 36 (LO RT), Maurizio Cattelan, "America," 2016/Kris McKay © Solomon R. Guggenheim Foundation; 37, xingmin07/GI; 39 (CTR RT), Edu Oliveros/iStockPhoto; 39 (LO RT), Eric Isselee/SS; 40 (LE), ESB Professional/SS; 40 (UP RT), cynoclub/GI; 40 (CTR RT), Madlen/SS; 41, E. O./SS; 42, Photo by Leemage/Corbis via GI; 43 (RT), The Chork Company; 44, Amawasri Pakdara/SS; 45 (UP), Piotr Naskreckl/Minden Pictures; 46, Photo: Peter Aaron/Architect: Adam Kalkin; 48 (UP), khuntong/SS; 48 (LO), Maxim Tupikov/SS; 49 (UP RT), Crafic; 50 (LO LE), Sueddeutsche Zeitung Photo/ASP; 51, Rolf Nussbaumer Photography/ASP; 52, Alain Grosclaude/AFP/GI; 54, OET/NautilusLive; 57, Fireball Printing; 58 (CTR), sabza/SS; 58 (LO LE), Hurst Photo/SS; 59 (UP LE), Rutchapong/GI; 59 (UP RT), Somchai Som/SS; 59 (LO CTR), mrkob/GI; 60, Dan Dennison/Hawaii Department of Land & Natural Resources; 62, Gary Sutton/Ocean Ecoventures; 64-65, Kanea/SS; 67, Patryk Kosmider/SS; 68, Courtesy Oliver Konter; 70-71, Andrea Izzotti/SS; 72, Mlenny/GI; 72 (LO RT), David Franklin/SS; 74 (LO RT), John Phillips/GI for JUST EAT; 75, www.4deserts.com/Onni Ca; 76-77, Cathy Keifer/SS; 78 (LE), Courtesy Paulo Miamoto; 78 (UP RT), Picture by Sean Berthiaume; 80, Universal History Archive/GI; 81, anossy Gergely/SS; 82-83, withGod/SS; 84, LifetimeStock/SS; 85, TTphoto/SS; 86, Grisha Bruev/SS; 88-89, Vlad61/SS; 90, Mark Olson, Traffic Crash Investigator, FCSO, COP division; 92, Robinson Photo/REX/SS; 93, Bill Roth/Adn/Alaska Dispatch News via Zuma Press; 94-95, Idaho Potato Commission; 97, Crown Copyright/Ministry of Defense; 98, Mass Poetry, 2016; 100, Photo by Will Sillin/Mike's Maze, Sunderland MA/2016; 103 (UP LE), MarcusVDT/SS; 103 (CTR RT), Vladimir Gjorgiev/SS; 103 (LO LE), Arvind Balaraman/SS; 104, Eric Isselee/Shutterstock; 105, Chelsea Lauren/GI; 106-107, igenkin/GI; 109, Lee Friesland; 110, Ian McAllister; 111 (UP), 2happy/SS; 111 (glasses), Nata-Lia/SS; 111 (collar), Tatyanaego/Dreamstime; 112, chert28/SS; 115, Alexander Semenov/Science Source; 116, Ocean Alliance/Whale.org; 117, Luo Yunfei/CNSPHOTO/VCG/GI; 118, Eric Isselee/SS; 120, Heartland Arts/SS; 123, Sean McCoy; 124-125, ALAMTX/ASP; 126, Fouroaks/Dreamstime; 127, Manila Social Club; 131, blickwinkel/ASP; 132, BRUSINI Aurlien/hemis.fr/GI; 133 (UP), Edward Kinsman/GI; 134, sumikophoto/SS; 135, Yann Hubert/SS; 136, cbimages/ASP; 138, Danita Delimont/GI; 139, Eric Vandevile/Gamma-Rapho via GI; 140, 2017 Royal Canadian Mint. All Rights Reserved; 141 (LO LE), Artville; 142-143, Jimmy Day/Courtesy MIT Media Lab; 144 (UP), alex5711/SS; 144 (LO RT), NASA/JPL/Northwestern University; 145, M. Kuntner; 146, NASA Images/SS; 147, KAMONRAT/SS; 148-149, Mike Veitch/Minden Pictures; 151, Rosa Jay/SS; 152, imagedj/SS; 152 (UP LE), Adrian Lubbers; 153 (UP RT), Bettmann/GI; 153 (CTR), terekhov igor/SS; 155-156, BonnieBC/SS; 157, Dipali S/SS; 158, Kletr/SS; 159, racorn/SS; 160, Fat Jackey/SS; 161, Boris Pamikov/SS; 163, Ericlefrancais/GI; 165, SWNS; 166-167, Bianca Lavies/National Geographic Creative; 168, NOAA OKEANOS EXPLORER Program, Oceano Profundo 2015; 169, Todd Wawrychuk/ABC via GI; 171, BIOSPHOTO/ASP; 173, Feature China/Barcroft Media Ltd.; 174, Bettmann/GI; 175, Jingle Johns; 176, Siberian Times; 177, Dr. Richard Beck; 178-179, Kalistratova/GI; 180, Tui De Roy/Minden Pictures; 180 (LO RT), Nito100/Dreamstime; 181 (LE), Thomas J. Sebourn/SS; 181 (RT), Patrick Van Tassell; 183, David Peart/GI; 184, gresei/SS; 184-185, M. Unal Ozmen/SS; 186, Courtesy Grand Canyon Caverns; 187, Reuters/Newscom; 188, Neal Cooper/Dreamstime; 189, Sky UK Limited/Andrea Southam; 190, Franco Tempesta; 192, US Army/GI; 193, mikeledray/SS; 194, Paul Fahy/REX/SS; 195, Water Environment & Reuse Foundation; 196, Tuzemka/SS; 197, Willee Cole/SS

Now YOU can be WEIRD 365 days a year!

This awesome daily planner is packed with fun facts, cool graphics, and plenty of space to write, doodle, and track assignments, activities, and get-togethers all year long.

NORWAY ONCE **KNIGHTED** A **PENGUIN** NAMED **SIR NILS OLAV.**

REPORTING FOR DUTY!

If you could name a penguin, what would you call it?

JANUARY 1
NEW YEAR'S DAY
MON | TUES | WED | THURS | FRI | SAT | SUN

2
MON | TUES | WED | THURS | FRI | SAT | SUN

MY GOALS FOR THIS MONTH

NATIONAL GEOGRAPHIC KiDS

weird but true! DAILY PLANNER
365 Days to Fill with School, Sports, Friends, and Fun!

NATIONAL GEOGRAPHIC KiDS

AVAILABLE WHEREVER BOOKS ARE SOLD • Get a fun freebie at **natgeokids.com/fun-pack**

Copyright © 2017 National Geographic Partners, LLC.